WAR IS A RACKET

WAR

IS A

RACKET

By

SMEDLEY D. BUTLER

Major General, United States Marines

(RETIRED)

CONTENTS

CHAPTER ONE

WAR IS A RACKET

War is a racket. It always has been. It is possibly the oldest, easily the most profitable, surely the most vicious. It is the only one international in scope. It is the only one in which the profits are reckoned in dollars and the losses in lives.

A racket is best described, I believe, as something that is not what it seems to the majority of people. Only a small "inside" group knows what it is about. It is conducted for the benefit of the very few, at the expense of the very many. Out of war a few people make huge fortunes.

In the World War a mere handful garnered the profits of the conflict. At least 21,000 new millionaires and billionaires were made in the United States during the World War. That many admitted their huge blood gains in their income tax returns. How many other war millionaires falsified their income tax returns no one knows.

How many of these war millionaires shouldered a rifle? How many of them dug a trench? How many of them knew what it meant to go hungry in a rat-infested dugout? How many of them spent sleepless, frightened nights, ducking shells and shrapnel and machine gun bullets? How many of them parried the bayonet thrust of an enemy? How many of them were wounded or killed in battle?

Out of war nations acquire additional territory, if they are victorious. They just take it. This newly acquired territory promptly is exploited by the few—the self-same few who wrung dollars out of blood in the war. The general public shoulders the bill.

And what is this bill?

This bill renders a horrible accounting. Newly placed gravestones. Mangled bodies. Shattered minds. Broken hearts and homes. Economic instability. Depression and all its attendant miseries. Back-breaking taxation for generations and generations.

For a great many years, as a soldier, I had a suspicion that war was a racket; not until I retired to civil life did I fully realize it. Now that I see the international war clouds again gathering, as they are today, I must face it and speak out.

Again they are choosing sides. France and Russia met and agreed to stand side by side. Italy and Austria hurried to make a similar agreement. Poland and Germany cast sheep's eyes at each other, forgetting, for the nonce, their dispute over the Polish Corridor. The assassination of King Alexander of Jugoslavia complicated matters. Jugoslavia and Hungary, long bitter enemies, were almost at each other's throats. Italy was ready to jump in. But France was waiting. So was Czechoslovakia. All of them are looking ahead to war. Not the people—not those who fight and pay and die—only those who foment wars and remain safely at home to profit.

There are 40,000,000 men under arms in the world today, and our statesmen and diplomats have the temerity to say that war is not in the making.

Hell's bells! Are these 40,000,000 men being trained to be dancers?

Not in Italy, to be sure. Premier Mussolini knows what they are being trained for. He, at least, is frank enough to speak out. Only the other day, Il Duce in "International Conciliation," the publication of the Carnegie Endowment for International Peace, said:

> "And above all, Fascism, the more it considers and observes the future and the development of humanity quite apart from political considerations of the moment, believes neither in the possibility nor the utility of perpetual peace.... War alone brings up to its highest tension all human energy and puts the stamp of nobility upon the peoples who have the courage to meet it."

Undoubtedly Mussolini means exactly what he says. His well trained army, his great fleet of planes, and even his navy are ready for war—anxious for it, apparently. His recent stand at the side of Hungary in the latter's dispute with Jugoslavia showed that. And the hurried mobilization of his troops on the Austrian border after the assassination of Dollfuss showed it too. There are others in Europe too whose sabre rattling presages war, sooner or later.

Herr Hitler, with his rearming Germany and his constant demands for more and more arms, is an equal if not a greater menace to peace. France only recently increased the term of military service for its youth from a year to eighteen months.

Yes, all over, nations are camping on their arms. The mad dogs of Europe are on the loose.

In the Orient the maneuvering is more adroit. Back in 1904, when Russia and

Japan fought, we kicked out our old friends the Russians and backed Japan. Then our very generous international bankers were financing Japan. Now the trend is to poison us against the Japanese. What does the "open door" policy in China mean to us? Our trade with China is about $90,000,000 a year. Or the Philippine Islands? We have spent about $600,000,000 in the Philippines in thirty-five years and we (our bankers and industrialists and speculators) have private investments there of less than $200,000,000.

Then, to save that China trade of about $90,000,000, or to protect these private investments of less than $200,000,000 in the Philippines, we would be all stirred up to hate Japan and to go to war—a war that might well cost us tens of billions of dollars, hundreds of thousands of lives of Americans, and many more hundreds of thousands of physically maimed and mentally unbalanced men.

Of course, for this loss, there would be a compensating profit—fortunes would be made. Millions and billions of dollars would be piled up. By a few. Munitions makers. Bankers. Ship builders. Manufacturers. Meat packers. Speculators. They would fare well.

Yes, they are getting ready for another war. Why shouldn't they? It pays high dividends.

But what does it profit the masses?

What does it profit the men who are killed? What does it profit the men who are maimed? What does it profit their mothers and sisters, their wives and their sweethearts? What does it profit their children?

What does it profit anyone except the very few to whom war means huge profits?

Yes, and what does it profit the nation?

Take our own case. Until 1898 we didn't own a bit of territory outside the mainland of North America. At that time our national debt was a little more than $1,000,000,000. Then we became "internationally minded." We forgot, or shunted aside, the advice of the Father of our Country. We forgot Washington's warning about "entangling alliances." We went to war. We acquired outside territory. At the end of the World War period, as a direct result of our fiddling in international affairs, our national debt had jumped to over $25,000,000,000. Our total favorable trade balance during the twenty-five-year period was about $24,000,000,000. Therefore, on a purely financial bookkeeping basis, we ran a little behind year for year, and that foreign trade might well have been ours without the wars.

It would have been far cheaper (not to say safer) for the average American who pays the bills to stay out of foreign entanglements. For a very few this racket, like bootlegging and other underworld rackets, brings fancy profits, but the cost of operations is always transferred to the people—who do not profit.

CHAPTER TWO

WHO

MAKES THE PROFITS?

The World War, rather our brief participation in it, has cost the United States some $52,000,000,000. Figure it out. That means $400 to every American man, woman, and child. And we haven't paid the debt yet. We are paying it, our children will pay it, and our children's children probably still will be paying the cost of that war.

The normal profits of a business concern in the United States are six, eight, ten, and sometimes even twelve per cent. But war-time profits—ah! that is another matter—twenty, sixty, one hundred, three hundred, and even eighteen hundred per cent—the sky is the limit. All that the traffic will bear. Uncle Sam has the money. Let's get it.

Of course, it isn't put that crudely in war time. It is dressed into speeches about patriotism, love of country, and "we must all put our shoulders to the wheel," but the profits jump and leap and skyrocket—and are safely pocketed. Let's just take a few examples:

Take our friends the du Ponts, the powder people—didn't one of them testify before a Senate committee recently that their powder won the war? Or saved the world for democracy? Or something? How did they do in the war? They were a patriotic corporation. Well, the average earnings of the du Ponts for the period 1910 to 1914 were $6,000,000 a year. It wasn't much, but the du Ponts managed to get along on it. Now let's look at their average yearly profit during the war years, 1914 to 1918. Fifty-eight million dollars a year profit, we find! Nearly ten times that of normal times, and the profits of normal times were pretty good. An increase in profits of more than 950 per cent.

Take one of our little steel companies that so patriotically shunted aside the making of rails and girders and bridges to manufacture war materials. Well, their 1910-1914 yearly earnings averaged $6,000,000. Then came the war. And, like loyal citizens, Bethlehem Steel promptly turned to munitions making. Did their profits jump—or did they let Uncle Sam in for a bargain? Well, their 1914-1918 average was $49,000,000 a year!

Or, let's take United States Steel. The normal earnings during the five-year period prior to the war were $105,000,000 a year. Not bad. Then along came the war and up went the profits. The average yearly profit for the period 1914-1918 was $240,000,000. Not bad.

There you have some of the steel and powder earnings. Let's look at something else. A little copper, perhaps. That always does well in war times.

Anaconda, for instance. Average yearly earnings during the pre-war years 1910-

1914 of $10,000,000. During the war years 1914-1918 profits leaped to $34,000,000 per year.

Or Utah Copper. Average of $5,000,000 per year during the 1910-1914 period. Jumped to average of $21,000,000 yearly profits for the war period.

Let's group these five, with three smaller companies. The total yearly average profits of the pre-war period 1910-1914 were $137,480,000. Then along came the war. The yearly average profits for this group skyrocketed to $408,300,000.

A little increase in profits of approximately 200 per cent.

Does war pay? It paid them. But they aren't the only ones. There are still others. Let's take leather.

For the three-year period before the war the total profits of Central Leather Company were $3,500,000. That was approximately $1,167,000 a year. Well, in 1916 Central Leather returned a profit of

$15,500,000, a small increase of 1,100 per cent. That's all. The General Chemical Company averaged a profit for the three years before the war of a little over $800,000 a year. Came the war, and the profits jumped to $12,000,000. A leap of 1,400 per cent.

International Nickel Company—and you can't have a war without nickel—showed an increase in profits from a mere average of $4,000,000 a year to $73,500,000 yearly. Not bad? An increase of more than 1,700 per cent.

American Sugar Refining Company averaged $2,000,000 a year for the three years before the war. In 1916 a profit of $6,000,000 was recorded.

Listen to Senate Document No. 259. The Sixty-Fifth Congress, reporting on corporate earnings and government revenues. Considering the profits of 122 meat packers, 153 cotton manufacturers, 299 garment makers, 49 steel plants, and 340 coal producers during the war. Profits under 25 per cent were exceptional. For instance, the coal companies made between 100 per cent and 7,856 per cent on their capital stock during the war. The Chicago packers doubled and tripled their earnings.

And let us not forget the bankers who financed this great war. If anyone had the cream of the profits it was the bankers. Being partnerships rather than incorporated organizations, they do not have to report to stockholders. And their profits were as secret as they were immense. How the bankers made their millions and their billions I do not know, because those little secrets never become public—even before a Senate investigatory body.

But here's how some of the other patriotic industrialists and speculators chiseled their way into war profits.

Take the shoe people. They like war. It brings business with abnormal profits. They made huge profits on sales abroad to our allies. Perhaps, like the munitions manufacturers and armament makers, they also sold to the enemy. For a dollar is a dollar whether it comes from Germany or from France. But they did well by Uncle Sam too. For instance, they sold Uncle Sam 35,000,000 pairs of hobnailed service shoes. There were 4,000,000 soldiers. Eight pairs, and more, to a soldier. My regiment during the war had only a pair to a soldier. Some of these shoes probably are still in existence. They were good shoes. But when the war was over Uncle Sam had a matter of 25,000,000 pairs left over. Bought—and paid for. Profits recorded and pocketed.

There was still lots of leather left. So the leather people sold your Uncle Sam hundreds of thousands of McClellan saddles for the cavalry. But there wasn't any American cavalry overseas! Somebody had to get rid of this leather, however. Somebody had to make a profit on it—so we had a lot of McClellan saddles. And we probably have those yet.

Also somebody had a lot of mosquito netting. They sold your Uncle Sam 20,000,000 mosquito nets for the use of the soldiers overseas. I suppose the boys were expected to put it over them as they tried to sleep in the muddy trenches—one hand scratching cooties on their backs and the other making passes at scurrying rats. Well, not one of these mosquito nets ever got to France!

Anyhow, these thoughtful manufacturers wanted to make sure that no soldier would be without his mosquito net, so 40,000,000 additional yards of mosquito netting were sold to Uncle Sam.

There were pretty good profits in mosquito netting in war days, even if there were no mosquitoes in France.

I suppose, if the war had lasted just a little longer, the enterprising mosquito netting manufacturers would have sold your Uncle Sam a couple of consignments of mosquitoes to plant in France so that more mosquito netting would be in order.

Airplane and engine manufacturers felt they, too, should get their just profits out of this war. Why not? Everybody else was getting theirs. So $1,000,000,000—count them if you live long enough—was spent by Uncle Sam in building airplanes and airplane engines that never left the ground! Not one plane, or motor, out of the billion dollars' worth ordered, ever got into a battle in France. Just the same the manufacturers made their little profit of 30, 100, or perhaps 300 per cent.

Undershirts for soldiers cost 14¢ to make and Uncle Sam paid 30¢ to 40¢ each for them—a nice little profit for the undershirt manufacturer. And the stocking manufacturers and the uniform manufacturers and the cap manufacturers and the steel helmet manufacturers—all got theirs.

Why, when the war was over some 4,000,000 sets of equipment—knapsacks and the things that go to fill them— crammed warehouses on this side. Now they are being scrapped because the regulations have changed the contents. But the manufacturers collected their wartime profits on them—and they will do it all over again the next time.

There were lots of brilliant ideas for profit making during the war.

One very versatile patriot sold Uncle Sam twelve dozen 48-inch wrenches. Oh, they were very nice wrenches. The only trouble was that there was only one nut ever made that was large enough for these wrenches. That is the one that holds the turbines at Niagara Falls! Well, after Uncle Sam had bought them and the manufacturer had pocketed the profit, the wrenches were put on freight cars and shunted all around the United States in an effort to find a use for them. When the Armistice was signed it was indeed a sad blow to the wrench manufacturer. We was just about to make some nuts to fit the wrenches. Then he planned to sell these, too, to your Uncle Sam.

Still another had the brilliant idea that colonels shouldn't ride in automobiles, nor should they even ride horseback. One had probably seen a picture of Andy Jackson riding on a buckboard. Well, some 6,000 buckboards were sold to Uncle Sam for the use of colonels! Not one of them was used. But the buckboard manufacturer got his war profit.

The shipbuilders felt they should come in on some of it, too. They built a lot of ships that made a lot of profit. More than $3,000,000,000 worth. Some of the ships were all right. But $635,000,000 worth of them were made of wood and wouldn't float! The seams opened up—and they sank. We paid for them, though. And somebody pocketed the profits.

It has been estimated by statisticians and economists and researchers that the war cost your Uncle Sam $52,000,000,000. Of this sum, $39,000,000,000 was expended in the actual war period. This expenditure yielded $16,000,000,000 in profits. That is how the 21,000 billionaires and millionaires got that way. This $16,000,000,000 profits is not to be sneezed at. It is quite a tidy sum. And it went to a very few.

The Senate (Nye) committee probe of the munitions industry and its wartime profits, despite its sensational disclosures, hardly has scratched the surface.

Even so, it has had some effect. The State Department has been studying "for some time" methods of keeping out of war. The War Department suddenly decides it has a wonderful plan to spring. The Administration names a committee—with the War and Navy Departments ably represented under the chairmanship of a Wall Street speculator—to limit profits in war time. To what extent isn't suggested. Hmmm. Possibly the profits of 300 and 600 and 1,600 per cent of those who turned blood into gold in the World War would be limited to some smaller figure.

Apparently, however, the plan does not call for any limitation of losses—that is, the losses of those who fight the war. As far as I have been able to ascertain there is nothing in the scheme to limit a soldier to the loss of but one eye, or one arm, or to limit his wounds to one or two or three. Or to limit the loss of life.

There is nothing in this scheme, apparently, that says not more than 12 per cent of a regiment shall be wounded in battle, or that not more than 7 per cent in a division shall be killed.

Of course, the committee cannot be bothered with such trifling matters.

CHAPTER THREE

WHO

PAYS THE BILLS?

Who provides the profits— these nice little profits of 20, 100, 300, 1,500, and 1,800 per cent? We all pay them—in taxation. We paid the bankers their profits when we bought Liberty Bonds at $100 and sold them back at $84 or $86 to the bankers. These bankers collected $100 plus. It was a simple manipulation. The bankers control the security marts. It was easy for them to depress the price of these bonds. Then all of us—the people—got frightened and sold the bonds at $84 or $86. The bankers bought them. Then these same bankers stimulated a boom and government bonds went to par—and above. Then the bankers collected their profits.

But the soldier pays the biggest part of the bill.

If you don't believe this, visit the American cemeteries on the battlefields abroad. Or visit any of the veterans' hospitals in the United States. On a tour of the country, in the midst of which I am at the time of this writing, I have visited eighteen government hospitals for veterans. In them are a total of about 50,000 destroyed men—men who were the pick of the nation eighteen years ago. The very able chief surgeon at the government hospital at Milwaukee, where there are 3,800 of the living dead, told me that mortality among veterans is three times as great as among those who stayed at home.

Boys with a normal viewpoint were taken out of the fields and offices and factories and classrooms and put into the ranks. There they were remolded; they were made over; they were made to "about face"; to regard murder as the order of the day. They were put shoulder to shoulder and, through mass psychology, they were entirely changed. We used them for a couple of years and trained them to think nothing at all of killing or of being killed.

Then, suddenly, we discharged them and told them to make another "about face"! This time they had to do their own readjusting, sans mass psychology, sans officers' aid and advice, sans nation-wide propaganda. We didn't need them any more. So we scattered them about without any "three-minute" or "Liberty Loan" speeches or parades. Many, too many, of these fine young boys are eventually destroyed, mentally, because they could not make that final "about face" alone.

In the government hospital at Marion, Indiana, 1,800 of these boys are in pens! Five hundred of them in a barracks with steel bars and wires all around outside the buildings and on the porches. These already have been mentally destroyed. These boys don't even look like human beings. Oh, the looks on their faces!

Physically, they are in good shape; mentally, they are gone.

There are thousands and thousands of these cases, and more and more are coming in all the time. The tremendous excitement of the war, the sudden cutting off of that excitement—the young boys couldn't stand it.

That's a part of the bill. So much for the dead—they have paid their part of the war profits. So much for the mentally and physically wounded—they are paying now their share of the war profits. But the others paid, too—they paid with heartbreaks when they tore themselves away from their firesides and their families to don the uniform of Uncle Sam—on which a profit had been made. They paid another part in the training camps where they were regimented and drilled while others took their jobs and their places in the lives of their communities. They paid for it in the trenches where they shot and were shot; where they went hungry for days at a time; where they slept in the mud and in the cold and in the rain—with the moans and shrieks of the dying for a horrible lullaby.

But don't forget—the soldier paid part of the dollars and cents bill too.

Up to and including the Spanish-American War, we had a prize system, and soldiers and sailors fought for money. During the Civil War they were paid bonuses, in many instances, before they went into service. The government, or states, paid as high as $1,200 for an enlistment. In the Spanish-American War they gave prize money. When we captured any vessels, the soldiers all got their share—at least, they were supposed to. Then it was found that we could reduce the cost of wars by taking all the prize money and keeping it, but conscripting the soldier anyway. Then the soldiers couldn't bargain for their labor. Everyone else could bargain, but the soldier couldn't.

Napoleon once said,

"All men are enamored of decorations ... they positively hunger for them."

So, by developing the Napoleonic system—the medal business—the government learned it could get soldiers for less money, because the boys liked to be decorated. Until the Civil War there were no medals. Then the Congressional Medal of Honor was handed out. It made enlistments easier. After the Civil War no new medals were issued until the Spanish-American War.

In the World War, we used propaganda to make the boys accept conscription. They were made to feel ashamed if they didn't join the army.

So vicious was this war propaganda that even God was brought into it. With few exceptions our clergymen joined in the clamor to kill, kill, kill. To kill the Germans. God is on our side ... it is His will that the Germans be killed.

And in Germany, the good pastors called upon the Germans to kill the allies

... to please the same God. That was a part of the general propaganda, built up to make people war conscious and murder conscious.

Beautiful ideals were painted for our boys who were sent out to die. This was the "war to end wars." This was the "war to make the world safe for democracy." No one told them that dollars and cents were the real reason. No one mentioned to them, as they marched away, that their going and their dying would mean huge war profits. No one told these American soldiers that they might be shot down by bullets made by their own brothers here. No one told them that the ships on which they were going to cross might be torpedoed by submarines built with United States patents. They were just told it was to be a "glorious adventure."

Thus, having stuffed patriotism down their throats, it was decided to make them help pay for the war, too. So, we gave them the large salary of $30 a month!

All they had to do for this munificent sum was to leave their dear ones behind, give up their jobs, lie in swampy trenches, eat canned willy (when they could get it) and kill and kill and kill ... and be killed.

But wait!

Half of that wage (just a little more in a month than a riveter in a shipyard or a laborer in a munitions factory safe at home made in a day) was promptly taken from him to support his dependents, so that they would not become a charge upon his community. Then we made him pay what amounted to accident insurance—something the employer pays for in an enlightened state—and that cost him $6 a month. He had less than $9 a month left.

Then, the most crowning insolence of all—he was virtually blackjacked into paying for his own ammunition, clothing, and food by being made to buy Liberty Bonds. Most soldiers got no money at all on pay days.

We made them buy Liberty Bonds at $100 and then we bought them back—when they came back from the war and couldn't find work—at $84 and $86. And the soldiers bought about $2,000,000,000 worth of these bonds!

Yes, the soldier pays the greater part of the bill. His family pays it too. They pay it in the same heart-break that he does. As he suffers, they suffer. At nights, as he lay in the trenches and watched shrapnel burst about him, they lay home in their beds and tossed sleeplessly—his father, his mother, his wife, his sisters, his brothers, his sons, and his daughters.

When he returned home minus an eye, or minus a leg or with his mind broken, they suffered too—as much as and even sometimes more than he. Yes, and they, too, contributed their dollars to the profits that the munitions makers and bankers and ship-builders and the manufacturers and the speculators made. They, too, bought Liberty Bonds and contributed to the profit of the bankers after the

Armistice in the hocus-pocus of manipulated Liberty Bond prices.

And even now the families of the wounded men and of the mentally broken and those who never were able to readjust themselves are still suffering and still paying.

CHAPTER FOUR

HOW TO SMASH
THIS
RACKET!

Well, it's a racket, all right.

A few profit—and the many pay.

But there is a way to stop it. You can't end it by disarmament conferences. You can't eliminate it by peace parleys at Geneva. Well-meaning but impractical groups can't wipe it out by resolutions. It can be smashed effectively only by taking the profit out of war.

The only way to smash this racket is to conscript capital and industry and labor before the nation's manhood can be conscripted. One month before the Government can conscript the young men of the nation—it must conscript capital and industry and labor. Let the officers and the directors and the high-powered executives of our armament factories and our steel companies and our munitions makers and our ship-builders and our airplane builders and the manufacturers of all the other things that provide profit in war time as well as the bankers and the speculators, be conscripted—to get $30 a month, the same wage as the lads in the trenches get.

Let the workers in these plants get the same wages—all the workers, all presidents, all executives, all directors, all managers, all bankers—yes, and all generals and all admirals and all officers and all politicians and all government office holders—everyone in the nation be restricted to a total monthly income not to exceed that paid to the soldier in the trenches!

Let all these kings and tycoons and masters of business and all those workers in industry and all our senators and governors and mayors pay half of their monthly $30 wage to their families and pay war risk insurance and buy Liberty Bonds.

Why shouldn't they?

They aren't running any risk of being killed or of having their bodies mangled or their minds shattered. They aren't sleeping in muddy trenches. They aren't hungry. The soldiers are!

Give capital and industry and labor thirty days to think it over and you will find, by that time, there will be no war. That will smash the war racket—that and nothing else.

Maybe I am a little too optimistic. Capital still has some say. So capital won't permit the taking of the profit out of war until the people—those who do the suffering and still pay the price—make up their minds that those they elect to office shall do their bidding, and not that of the profiteers.

Another step necessary in this fight to smash the war racket is a limited plebiscite to determine whether war should be declared. A plebiscite not of all the voters but merely of those who would be called upon to do the fighting and the dying. There wouldn't be very much sense in having the 76-year-old president of a munitions factory or the flat-footed head of an international banking firm or the cross-eyed manager of a uniform manufacturing plant—all of whom see visions of tremendous profits in the event of war—voting on whether the nation should go to war or not. They never would be called upon to shoulder arms— to sleep in a trench and to be shot. Only those who would be called upon to risk their lives for their country should have the privilege of voting to determine whether the nation should go to war.

There is ample precedent for restricting the voting to those affected. Many of our states have restrictions on those permitted to vote. In most, it is necessary to be able to read and write before you may vote. In some, you must own property. It would be a simple matter each year for the men coming of military age to register in their communities as they did in the draft during the World War and to be examined physically. Those who could pass and who would therefore be called upon to bear arms in the event of war would be eligible to vote in a limited plebiscite. They should be the ones to have the power to decide— and not a Congress few of whose members are within the age limit and fewer still of whom are in physical condition to bear arms. Only those who must suffer should have the right to vote.

A third step in this business of smashing the war racket is to make certain that our military forces are truly forces for defense only.

At each session of Congress the question of further naval appropriations comes up. The swivel-chair admirals of Washington (and there are always a lot of them) are very adroit lobbyists. And they are smart. They don't shout that "We need a lot of battleships to war on this nation or that nation." Oh, no. First of all, they let it be known that America is menaced by a great naval power. Almost any day, these admirals will tell you, the great fleet of this supposed enemy will strike suddenly and annihilate our 125,000,000 people. Just like that. Then they begin to cry for a larger navy. For what? To fight the enemy? Oh my, no. Oh, no. For defense purposes only.

Then, incidentally, they announce maneuvers in the Pacific. For defense. Uh, huh.

The Pacific is a great big ocean. We have a tremendous coastline on the Pacific. Will the maneuvers be off the coast, two or three hundred miles? Oh, no. The maneuvers will be two thousand, yes, perhaps even thirty-five hundred miles, off the coast.

The Japanese, a proud people, of course will be pleased beyond expression to see the United States fleet so close to Nippon's shores. Even as pleased as would be the residents of California were they to dimly discern, through the morning mist, the Japanese fleet playing at war games off Los Angeles.

The ships of our navy, it can be seen, should be specifically limited, by law, to within 200 miles of our coastline. Had that been the law in 1898 the Maine would never have gone to Havana Harbor. She never would have been blown up. There would have been no war with Spain with its attendant loss of life. Two hundred miles is ample, in the opinion of experts, for defense purposes. Our nation cannot start an offensive war if its ships can't go farther than 200 miles from the coastline. Planes might be permitted to go as far as 500 miles from the coast for purposes of reconnaissance. And the army should never leave the territorial limits of our nation.

To summarize: Three steps must be taken to smash the war racket.

We must take the profit out of war.

We must permit the youth of the land who would bear arms to decide whether or not there should be war.

We must limit our military forces to home defense purposes.

CHAPTER FIVE

TO HELL WITH

WAR!

I am not such a fool as to believe that war is a thing of the past. I know the people do not want war, but there is no use in saying we cannot be pushed into another war.

Looking back, Woodrow Wilson was re-elected president in 1916 on a platform that he had "kept us out of war" and on the implied promise that he would "keep us out of war." Yet, five months later he asked Congress to declare war on Germany.

In that five-month interval the people had not been asked whether they had changed their minds. The 4,000,000 young men who put on uniforms and marched or sailed away were not asked whether they wanted to go forth to suffer and to die.

Then what caused our government to change its mind so suddenly?

Money.

An allied commission, it may be recalled, came over shortly before the war declaration and called on the President. The President summoned a group of advisers. The head of the commission spoke. Stripped of its diplomatic language, this is what he told the President and his group:

> "There is no use kidding ourselves any longer. The cause of the allies is lost. We now owe you (American bankers, American munitions makers, American manufacturers, American speculators, American exporters) five or six billion dollars.
> "If we lose (and without the help of the United States we must lose) we, England, France and Italy, cannot pay back this money ... and Germany won't.
> "So...."

Had secrecy been outlawed as far as war negotiations were concerned, and had the press been invited to be present at that conference, or had the radio been available to broadcast the proceedings, America never would have entered the World War. But this conference, like all war discussions, was shrouded in the utmost secrecy.

When our boys were sent off to war they were told it was a "war to make the world safe for democracy" and a "war to end all wars."

Well, eighteen years after, the world has less of democracy than it had then. Besides, what business is it of ours whether Russia or Germany or England or France or Italy or Austria live under democracies or monarchies? Whether they are Fascists or Communists? Our problem is to preserve our own democracy.

And very little, if anything, has been accomplished to assure us that the World War was really the war to end all wars.

Yes, we have had disarmament conferences and limitations of arms conferences. They don't mean a thing. One has just failed; the results of another have been nullified. We send our professional soldiers and our sailors and our politicians and our diplomats to these conferences. And what happens?

The professional soldiers and sailors don't want to disarm. No admiral wants to be without a ship. No general wants to be without a command. Both mean men without jobs. They are not for disarmament. They cannot be for limitations of arms. And at all these conferences, lurking in the background but all-powerful, just the same, are the sinister agents of those who profit by war. They see to it that these conferences do not disarm or seriously limit armaments.

The chief aim of any power at any of these conferences has been not to achieve disarmament in order to prevent war but rather to endeavor to get more armament for itself and less for any potential foe.

There is only one way to disarm with any semblance of practicability. That is for all nations to get together and scrap every ship, every gun, every rifle, every tank, every war plane. Even this, if it were at all possible, would not be enough.

The next war, according to experts, will be fought not with battleships, not by artillery, not with rifles and not with machine guns. It will be fought with deadly chemicals and gases.

Secretly each nation is studying and perfecting newer and ghastlier means of annihilating its foes wholesale. Yes, ships will continue to be built, for the shipbuilders must make their profits. And guns still will be manufactured and powder and rifles will be made, for the munitions makers must make their huge profits. And the soldiers, of course, must wear uniforms, for the manufacturers must make their war profits too.

But victory or defeat will be determined by the skill and ingenuity of our scientists.

If we put them to work making poison gas and more and more fiendish mechanical and explosive instruments of destruction, they will have no time for the constructive job of building a greater prosperity for all peoples. By putting them to this useful job, we can all make more money out of peace than we can out of war—even the munition makers.

So ... I say,

"TO HELL WITH WAR!"

SMEDLEY

DARLINGTON BUTLER

S medley Darlington Butler was born July 30, 1881, in West Chester, Pennsylvania, the eldest of three sons. His parents, Thomas and Maud (née Darlington) Butler, were descended from local Quaker families. Both of his parents were of entirely English ancestry, all of whom had been in North America since the 17th century. His father was a lawyer, a judge and later served in the House of Representatives for 31 years, serving as chairman of the House Naval Affairs Committee during the Harding and Coolidge administrations. Smedley's Marine Corps career successes occurred while his father held that politically influential Congressional seat controlling the Marine Corps manpower and budget.

His maternal grandfather was Smedley Darlington, a Republican congressman from 1887 to 1891.

Butler attended the West Chester Friends Graded High School, followed by The Haverford School, a secondary school popular with sons of upper-class Philadelphia families. He became captain of the school baseball team and quarterback of its football team. Against the wishes of his father, he left school 38 days before his seventeenth birthday to enlist in the Marine Corps during the Spanish–American War. Nevertheless, Haverford awarded him his high school diploma on June 6, 1898, before the end of his final year. His transcript stated that he completed the scientific course "with Credit".

In the Spanish war fervor of 1898, Butler lied about his age to receive a direct commission as a Marine second lieutenant. He trained at Marine Barracks, Washington, D.C. In July 1898, he went to Guantánamo Bay, Cuba, arriving shortly after its invasion and capture. His company soon returned to the U.S., and after a short break he was assigned to the armored cruiser USS *New York* for four months. He came home to be mustered out of service in February 1899, but on April 8, 1899, he accepted a commission as a first lieutenant in the Marine Corps.

The Marine Corps sent him to Manila, Philippines. On garrison duty with little to do, Butler turned to alcohol to relieve the boredom. He once became drunk and was temporarily relieved of command after an unspecified incident in his room.

In October 1899, he saw his first combat action when he led 300 Marines to take the town of Noveleta from Filipino troops of the new Philippine republic. In the initial moments of the assault, his first sergeant was wounded. Butler briefly panicked but quickly regained his composure and led his Marines in pursuit of the fleeing enemy. By noon, the Marines had dispersed the native defenders and taken the town. One

Marine had been killed, and ten were wounded. Another 50 Marines had been incapacitated by the humid tropical heat.

After the excitement of this combat, garrison duty again became routine. He met Littleton Waller, a fellow Marine with whom he maintained a lifelong friendship. When Waller received command of a company in Guam, he was allowed to select five officers to take with him. Butler was amongst his choices. Before they had departed, their orders were changed, and they were sent to China aboard the USS *Solace* to help put down the Boxer Rebellion.

Once in China, Butler was initially deployed at Tientsin. He took part in the Battle of Tientsin on July 13, 1900, and in the subsequent Gaselee Expedition, during which he saw the mutilated remains of Japanese soldiers. When he saw another Marine officer fall wounded, he climbed out of a trench to rescue him. Butler was then shot in the thigh. Another Marine helped him get to safety but also was shot. Despite his leg wound, Butler assisted the wounded officer to the rear. Four enlisted men would receive the Medal of Honor in the battle. Butler's commanding officer, Major Waller, personally commended him and wrote that "for such reward as you may deem proper the following officers: Lieutenant Smedley D. Butler, for the admirable control of his men in all the fights of the week, for saving a wounded man at the risk of his own life, and under a very severe fire." Commissioned officers were not then eligible to receive the Medal of Honor, and Butler instead received a promotion to captain by brevet while he recovered in the hospital, two weeks before his 19th birthday.

He was eligible for the Marine Corps Brevet Medal when it was created in 1921, and was one of only 20 Marines to receive it. His citation reads:

The Secretary of the Navy takes pleasure in transmitting to First Lieutenant Smedley Darlington Butler, United States

Marine Corps, the Brevet Medal which is awarded in accordance with Marine Corps Order No. 26 (1921), for distinguished conduct and public service in the presence of the enemy while serving with the Second Battalion of Marines, near Tientsin, China, on 13 July 1900. On 28 March 1901, First Lieutenant Butler is appointed Captain by brevet, to take rank from 13 July 1900.

Butler participated in a series of occupations, "police actions" and interventions by the United States in Central America and the Caribbean, later called the Banana Wars because their goal was to protect American commercial interests in the region, particularly those of the United Fruit Company. This company had significant financial stakes in the production of bananas, tobacco, sugar cane, and other products throughout the Caribbean, Central America, and the northern portions of South America. The U.S. was also trying to advance its own political interests by maintaining its influence in the region and especially its control of the Panama Canal. These interventions started with the Spanish–American War in 1898 and ended with the withdrawal of troops from Haiti and President Franklin D. Roosevelt's Good Neighbor policy in 1934. After his retirement, Butler became an outspoken critic of the business interests in the Caribbean, criticizing the ways in which American businesses and Wall Street bankers imposed their agenda on U.S. foreign policy during this period.

In 1903, Butler was stationed in Puerto Rico on Culebra Island. Hearing rumors of a Honduran revolt, the United States government ordered his unit and a supporting naval detachment to sail to Honduras, 1,500 miles (2,414 km) to the west, to defend the U.S. Consulate there. Using a converted banana boat renamed the *Panther*, Butler and several hundred Marines landed at the port town of Puerto Cortés. In a letter home, he describes the action: they were "prepared to land and shoot everybody and everything that was breaking the peace", but instead found a quiet town. The Marines re-boarded the *Panther* and continued up the coast line, looking for rebels at several towns, but found none.

When they arrived at Trujillo, however, they heard gunfire and came upon a battle in progress that had been ongoing for 55 hours between rebels called *Bonillista* and Honduran government soldiers at a local fort. At the sight of the Marines, the fighting ceased, and Butler led a detachment of Marines to the American consulate, where he found the consul, wrapped in an American flag, hiding among the floor beams. As soon as the Marines left the area with the shaken consul, the battle resumed, and the Bonillistas soon controlled the government. During this expedition Butler earned the first of his nicknames, "Old Gimlet Eye". It was attributed to his feverish, bloodshot eyes—he was suffering from some unnamed tropical fever at the time—that enhanced his penetrating and bellicose stare.

After the Honduran campaign, Butler returned to Philadelphia. He married Ethel Conway Peters of Philadelphia, a daughter of civil engineer and railroad executive Richard Peters, on June 30, 1905. His best man at the wedding was his former commanding officer in China, Lieutenant Colonel Littleton Waller. The couple eventually had three children: a daughter, Ethel Peters Butler, and two sons, Smedley Darlington Jr. and Thomas Richard.

Butler was next assigned to garrison duty in the Philippines, where he once launched a resupply mission across the stormy waters of Subic Bay after his isolated outpost ran out of rations. In 1908, he was diagnosed as having a nervous breakdown and received nine months sick leave, which he spent at home. He successfully managed a coal mine in West Virginia but returned to active duty in the Marine Corps at the first opportunity.

From 1909 to 1912 Butler served in Nicaragua enforcing U.S. policy. With a 104-degree fever, he led his battalion to the relief of the rebel-besieged city of Granada. In December 1909 he commanded the 3rd Battalion, 1st Marine Regiment on the Isthmus of Panama. On August 11, 1912, he was temporarily detached to command an expeditionary battalion he led in the Battle of Masaya on September 19, 1912, and the bombardment, assault and capture of Coyotepe Hill, Nicaragua in October 1912. He remained in Nicaragua until November 1912, when he rejoined the 3rd Battalion, 1st Marines at Camp Elliott, Panama.

Butler and his family were living in Panama in January 1914 when he was ordered to report as the Marine officer of a battleship squadron massing off the coast of Mexico, near Veracruz, to monitor a revolutionary movement. He did not like leaving his family and the home they had established in Panama and intended to request orders home as soon as he determined he was not needed.

On March 1, 1914, Butler and Navy Lieutenant Frank J. Fletcher (not to be confused with his uncle, Rear Admiral Frank F. Fletcher) "went ashore at Veracruz, where they met the American superintendent of the Inter-Oceanic Railway and surreptitiously rode in his private car [a railway car] up the line 75 miles to Jalapa and back". A purpose of the trip was to allow Butler and Fletcher to discuss the details of a future expedition into Mexico. Fletcher's plan required Butler to make his way into the country and develop a more detailed invasion plan while inside its borders. It was a spy mission and Butler was enthusiastic to get started. When Fletcher explained the plan to the commanders in Washington, DC, they agreed to it. Butler was given the go-ahead. A few days later he set out by train on his spy mission to

Mexico City, with a stopover at Puebla. He made his way to the U.S. Consulate in Mexico City, posing as a railroad official named "Mr. Johnson".

> *March 5.* As I was reading last night, waiting for dinner to be served, a visitant, rather than a visitor, appeared in my drawing-room *incognito* – a simple "Mr. Johnson," eager, intrepid, dynamic, efficient, unshaven!

He and the chief railroad inspector scoured the city, saying they were searching for a lost railroad employee; there was no lost employee, and in fact the employee they said was lost never existed. The ruse gave Butler access to various areas of the city. In the process of the so-called search, they located weapons in use by the Mexican army and determined the size of units and states of readiness. They updated maps and verified the railroad lines for use in an impending U.S. invasion. On March 7, 1914, he returned to Veracruz with the information he had gathered and presented it to his commanders. The invasion plan was eventually scrapped when authorities loyal to Mexican General Victoriano Huerta detained a small American naval landing party (that had gone ashore to buy gasoline) in Tampico, Mexico, which led to what became known as the Tampico Affair.

When President Woodrow Wilson discovered that an arms shipment was about to arrive in Mexico, he sent a contingent of Marines and sailors to Veracruz to intercept it on April 21, 1914. Over the next few days, street fighting and sniper fire posed a threat to Butler's force, but a door-to-door search rooted out most of the resistance. By April 26, the landing force of 5,800 Marines and sailors secured the city, which they held for the next six months. By the end of the conflict the Americans reported 17 dead and 63 wounded, and the Mexican forces had 126 dead and 195 wounded. After the actions at Veracruz, the U.S. decided to minimize the bloodshed and changed their plans from a full invasion of Mexico to simply maintaining the city of Veracruz. For his actions on April 22, Butler was awarded his first Medal of Honor. The citation reads:

For distinguished conduct in battle, engagement of Vera Cruz, 22 April 1914. Major Butler was eminent and conspicuous in command of his battalion. He exhibited courage and skill in leading his men through the action of the 22d and in the final occupation of the city.

After the occupation of Veracruz, many military personnel received the Medal of Honor, an unusually high number. The Army presented one, nine went to Marines and 46 were bestowed upon naval personnel. During World War I, Butler attempted to return his medal, explaining he had done nothing to deserve it. The medal was returned to him with orders to keep it and to wear it as well.

In 1915, Haitian President Vilbrun Guillaume Sam was killed by a mob. In response, the United States ordered the

USS *Connecticut* to Haiti with Major Butler and a group of Marines on board. On October 24, 1915, an estimated 400 *Cacos* ambushed Butler's patrol of 44 mounted Marines when they approached Fort Dipitie. Surrounded by *Cacos*, the Marines maintained their perimeter throughout the night. The next morning they charged the much larger enemy force by breaking out in three directions. The startled Haitians fled. In early November, Butler and a force of 700 Marines and sailors returned to the mountains to clear the area. At their temporary headquarters base at Le Trou they fought off an attack by about 100 *Cacos*. After the Americans took several other forts and ramparts during the following days, only Fort Rivière, an old French-built stronghold atop Montagne Noire, was left.

For the operation, Butler was given three companies of Marines and some sailors from the USS *Connecticut*, about 100 men. They encircled the fort and gradually closed in on it. Butler reached the fort from the southern side with the 15th Company and found a small opening in the wall. The Marines entered through the opening and engaged the *Cacos* in hand-to-hand combat. Butler and the Marines took the rebel stronghold on November 17, an action for which he received his second Medal of Honor, as well as the Haitian Medal of Honor. The entire battle lasted less than 20 minutes. Only one Marine was injured in the assault; he was struck by a rock and lost two teeth. All 51 Haitians in the fort were killed. Butler's exploits impressed Assistant Secretary of the Navy Franklin D. Roosevelt, who recommended the award based upon Butler's performance during the engagement. Once the medal was approved and presented in 1917, Butler achieved the distinction, shared with Dan Daly, of being the only Marines to receive the Medal of Honor twice for separate actions. The citation reads:

For extraordinary heroism in action as Commanding Officer of detachments from the 5th, 13th, 23d Companies and the Marine and sailor detachment from the U.S.S. Connecticut, Major Butler led the attack on Fort Rivière, Haiti, 17 November 1915. Following a concentrated drive, several different detachments of Marines gradually closed in on the old French bastion fort in an effort to cut off all avenues of retreat for the Caco bandits. Reaching the fort on the southern side where there was a small opening in the wall, Major Butler gave the signal to attack and Marines from the 15th Company poured through the breach, engaged the Cacos in hand-to-hand combat, took the bastion and crushed the Caco resistance. Throughout this perilous action, Major Butler was conspicuous for his bravery and forceful leadership.

Subsequently, as the initial organizer and commanding officer of the Gendarmerie d'Haïti, the native police force, Butler established a record as a capable administrator. Under his supervision, social order, administered by the dictatorship, was largely restored, and many vital public works projects were successfully completed. He recalled later that, during his time in Haiti, he and his troops "hunted the *Cacos* like pigs."

During World War I Butler was, to his disappointment, not assigned to a combat command on the Western Front. He made several requests for a posting in France, writing letters to his personal friend, Wendell Cushing Neville. While Butler's superiors considered him brave and brilliant, they described him as "unreliable."

In October 1918 he was promoted to the rank of brigadier general at the age of 37 and placed in command of Camp Pontanezen at Brest, France, a debarkation depot that funneled troops of the American Expeditionary Force to the battlefields. The camp had been unsanitary, overcrowded and disorganized. U.S. Secretary of War Newton Baker sent novelist Mary Roberts Rinehart to report on the camp. She later described how Butler tackled the sanitation problems. He began by solving the problem of mud: "[T]he ground under the tents was nothing but mud, [so] he had raided the wharf at Brest of the duckboards no longer needed for the trenches, carted the first one himself up that four-mile hill to the camp, and thus provided something in the way of protection for the men to sleep on." Gen. John J. Pershing authorized a duckboard shoulder patch for the units. This earned Butler another nickname, "Old Duckboard." For his exemplary service he was awarded both the Army Distinguished Service Medal and Navy Distinguished Service Medal and the French Order of the Black Star. The citation for the Army Distinguished Service Medal states:

The President of the United States of America, authorized by Act of Congress, July 9, 1918, takes pleasure in presenting the Army Distinguished Service Medal to Brigadier General Smedley Darlington

Butler, United States Marine Corps, for exceptionally meritorious and distinguished services to the Government of the United States, in a duty of great responsibility during World War I. Brigadier General Butler commanded with ability and energy Pontanezen Camp at Brest during the time in which it has developed into the largest embarkation camp in the world. Confronted with problems of extraordinary magnitude in supervising the reception, entertainment and departure of the large numbers of officers and soldiers passing through this camp, he has solved all with conspicuous success, performing services of the highest character for the American Expeditionary Forces.

The citation for the Navy Distinguished Service Medal states:

The President of the United States of America takes pleasure in presenting the Navy Distinguished Service Medal to Brigadier General Smedley Darlington Butler, United States Marine Corps, for exceptionally meritorious and distinguished services in France, during World War I. Brigadier General Butler organized, trained and commanded the 13th Regiment Marines; also the 5th Brigade of Marines. He commanded with ability and energy Camp Pontanezen at Brest during the time in which it has developed into the largest embarkation camp in the world. Confronted with problems of extraordinary magnitude in supervising the reception, entertainment and departure of large numbers of officers and soldiers passing through the camp, he has solved all with conspicuous success, performing services of the highest character for the American Expeditionary Forces.

Following the war, he became commanding general of the Marine barracks at Marine Corps Base Quantico, Virginia. At Quantico he transformed the wartime training camp into a permanent Marine post. He directed the Quantico camp's growth until it became the "showplace" of the Corps. Butler won national attention by taking thousands of his men on long field marches, many of which he led from the front, to Gettysburg and other Civil War battle sites, where they conducted large-scale re-enactments before crowds of distinguished spectators.

During a training exercise in western Virginia in 1921, he was told by a local farmer that Stonewall Jackson's arm was buried nearby, to which he replied, "Bosh! I will take a squad of Marines and dig up that spot to prove you wrong!" Butler found the arm in a box. He later replaced the wooden box with a metal one, and reburied the arm. He left a plaque on the granite monument marking the burial place of Jackson's arm; the plaque is no longer on the marker but can be viewed at the Chancellorsville Battlefield visitor's center.

In 1924 newly elected Mayor of Philadelphia W. Freeland Kendrick asked President Calvin Coolidge to lend the City a military general to help him rid Philadelphia's municipal government of crime and corruption. At the urging of Butler's father, Coolidge authorized Butler to take the necessary leave from the Corps to serve as Philadelphia's director of public safety in charge of running the city's police and fire departments from January 1924 until December 1925. He began his new job by assembling all 4,000 of the city police into the Metropolitan Opera House in shifts to introduce himself and inform them that things would change while he was in charge. Since he had not been given authority to fire corrupt police officers, he switched entire units from one part of the city to another, to undermine local protection rackets and profiteering.

Within 48 hours of taking over Butler organized raids on more than 900 speakeasies, ordering them padlocked and, in many cases, destroyed. In addition to raiding the speakeasies, he also attempted to eliminate other illegal activities: bootlegging, prostitution, gambling and police corruption. More zealous than he was political, he ordered crackdowns on the social elite's favorite hangouts, such as the Ritz-Carlton and the Union League, as well as on drinking establishments that served the working class. Although he was effective in reducing crime and police corruption, he was a controversial leader. In one instance he made a statement that he would promote the first officer to kill a bandit and stated, "I don't believe there is a single bandit notch on a policeman's guns [*sic*] in this city; go out and get some." Although many of the local citizens and police felt that the raids were just a show, they continued for several weeks.

He implemented programs to improve city safety and security. He established policies and guidelines of administration and developed a Philadelphia police uniform that resembled that of the Marine Corps. Other changes included military-style checkpoints into the city, bandit-chasing squads armed with sawed-off shotguns and armored police cars. The press began reporting on the good and the bad aspects of Butler's personal war on crime. The reports praised the new uniforms, the new programs and the reductions in crime but they also reflected the public's negative opinion of their new Public Safety Director. Many felt that he was being too aggressive in his tactics and resented the reductions in their civil rights, such as the stopping of citizens at the city checkpoints. Butler frequently swore in his radio addresses, causing many citizens to suggest his behavior, particularly his language, was inappropriate for someone of his rank and stature. Some even suggested Butler acted like a military dictator, even charging that he wrongfully used active-duty Marines in some of his raids. Maj. R.A. Haynes, the federal Prohibition commissioner, visited the city in 1924, six months after Butler was appointed. He announced that "great progress" had been made in the city and attributed that success to Butler.

Eventually Butler's leadership style and the directness of actions undermined his support within the community. His departure seemed imminent. Mayor Kendrick reported to the press, "I had the guts to bring General Butler to Philadelphia and I have the guts to fire him." Feeling that his duties in Philadelphia were coming to an end, Butler contacted Gen. Lejeune to prepare for his return to the Marine Corps. Not all of the city felt he was doing a bad job, though, and when the news started to leak that he would be leaving, people began to gather at the Academy of Music. A group of 4,000 supporters assembled and negotiated a truce between him and the mayor to keep him in Philadelphia for a while longer, and the president authorized a one-year extension.

Butler devoted much of his second year to executing arrest warrants, cracking down on crooked police and enforcing prohibition. On January 1, 1926, his leave from the Marine Corps ended and the president declined a request for a second extension. Butler received orders to report to San Diego and prepared his family and his belongings for the new assignment. In light of his pending departure, he began to defy the mayor and other key city officials. On the eve of his departure, he had an article printed in the paper stating his intention to stay and "finish the job". The mayor was surprised and furious when he read the press release the next morning and demanded his resignation. After almost two years in office, Butler resigned under pressure, stating later that "cleaning up Philadelphia was worse than any battle I was ever in."

Following the period of service as the director of public safety in Philadelphia, Butler assumed command on February 28, 1926, of the U.S. Marine Corps base in San Diego, California, in ceremonies involving officers and the band of the 4th Marine Regiment.

From 1927 to 1929 Butler was commander of a Marine Expeditionary

Force in Tientsin, China, (the China Marines). While there, he cleverly parlayed his influence among various generals and warlords to the protection of U.S. interests, ultimately winning the public acclaim of contending Chinese leaders. When he returned to the United States in 1929 he was promoted to major general, becoming, at age 48, the youngest major general of the Marine Corps. But the death of his father on 26 May 1928 ended the Pennsylvania Congressman's ability to protect Smedley from political retribution for his outspoken views.

In 1931 Butler violated diplomatic norms by publicly recounting gossip about Benito Mussolini in which the dictator allegedly struck and killed a child with his speeding automobile in a hit-and-run accident. The Italian government protested and President Hoover, who strongly disliked Butler, forced Secretary of the Navy Charles Francis Adams III to court-martial him. Butler became the first general officer to be placed under arrest since the Civil War. He apologized to Secretary Adams and the court-martial was canceled with only a reprimand.

When Commandant of the Marine Corps Maj. Gen. Wendell C. Neville died July 8, 1930, Butler, at that time the senior major general in the Corps, was a candidate for the position. Although he had significant support from many inside and outside the Corps, including John Lejeune and Josephus Daniels, two other Marine Corps generals were seriously considered—Ben H. Fuller and John H. Russell Jr.. Lejeune and others petitioned President Herbert Hoover, garnered support in the Senate and flooded Secretary of the Navy Charles Adams' desk with more than 2,500 letters of support. With the recent death of his influential father, however, Butler had lost much of his protection from his civilian superiors. The outspokenness that characterized his run-ins with the mayor of Philadelphia, the "unreliability" mentioned by his superiors when they were opposing Butler's posting to the Western Front, and his comments about Benito Mussolini resurfaced. In the end the position of commandant went to Fuller, who had more years of commissioned service than Butler and was considered less controversial. Butler requested retirement and left active duty on October 1, 1931.

Even before retiring from the Corps, Butler began developing his post-Corps career. In May 1931 he took part in a commission established by Oregon Governor Julius L. Meier which laid the foundations for the Oregon State Police. He began lecturing at events and conferences, and after his retirement from the Marines in 1931 he took this up full-time. He donated much of his earnings from his lucrative lecture circuits to the Philadelphia unemployment relief. He toured the western United States, making 60 speeches before returning for his daughter's marriage to Marine aviator Lt. John Wehle. Her wedding was the only time he wore his dress blue uniform after he left the Marines.

Butler announced his candidacy for the U.S. Senate in the Republican primary in Pennsylvania in March 1932 as a proponent of Prohibition, known as a "dry". Butler allied with Gifford Pinchot but was defeated in the April 26, 1932, primary election with only 37.5% of the vote to incumbent Sen. James J. Davis' 60%. A third candidate received the remainder of the votes. According to biographer Mark Strecker, Butler voted for Norman Thomas of the Socialist Party for president in 1936.

During his Senate campaign, Butler spoke out forcefully about the veterans' bonus. Veterans of World War I, many of whom had been out of work since the beginning of the Great Depression, sought immediate cash payment of Service Certificates granted to them eight years earlier via the World War Adjusted Compensation Act of 1924. Each Service Certificate, issued to a qualified veteran soldier, bore a face value equal to the soldier's promised payment, plus compound interest. The problem was that the certificates (like bonds), matured 20 years from the date of original issuance, thus, under extant law, the Service Certificates could not be redeemed until 1945. In June 1932, approximately 43,000 marchers—17,000 of whom were World War I veterans, their families, and affiliated groups—protested in Washington, D.C. The Bonus Expeditionary Force, also known as the "Bonus Army", marched on Washington to advocate the passage of the "soldier's bonus" for service during World War I. After Congress adjourned, bonus marchers remained in the city and became unruly. On July 28, 1932, two bonus marchers were shot by police, causing the entire mob to become hostile and riotous. The FBI, then known as the United States Bureau of Investigation, checked its fingerprint records to obtain the police records of individuals who had been arrested during the riots or who had participated in the bonus march.

The veterans made camp in the Anacostia flats while they awaited the congressional decision on whether or not to pay the bonus. The motion, known as the Patman bill, was decisively defeated, but the veterans stayed in their camp. On July 19 Butler arrived with his young son Thomas, the day before the official eviction by the Hoover administration. He walked through the camp and spoke to the veterans; he told them that they were fine soldiers and they had a right to lobby Congress just as much as any corporation. He and his son spent the night and ate with the men, and in the morning Butler gave a speech to the camping veterans. He instructed them to keep their sense of humor and cautioned them not to do anything that would cost public sympathy. On July 28, army cavalry units led by General Douglas MacArthur dispersed the Bonus Army by riding through it and using gas. During the conflict several veterans were killed or injured and Butler declared himself a "Hoover-for-Ex-President-Republican".

After his retirement and later years, Butler became widely known for his outspoken lectures against war profiteering, U.S. military adventurism, and what he viewed as nascent fascism in the United States.

In December 1933, Butler toured the country with James E. Van Zandt to recruit members for the Veterans of Foreign Wars (VFW). He described their effort as "trying to educate the soldiers out of the sucker class." In his speeches he denounced the Economy Act of 1933, called on veterans to organize politically to win their benefits, and condemned the FDR administration for its ties to big business. The VFW reprinted one of his speeches with the title "You Got to Get Mad" in its magazine *Foreign Service*. He said: "I believe in...taking Wall St. by the throat and shaking it up." He believed the rival veterans' group the American Legion was controlled by banking interests. On December 8, 1933, he said: "I have never known one leader of the American Legion who had never sold them out—and I mean it."

In addition to his speeches to pacifist groups, he served from 1935 to 1937 as a spokesman for the American League Against War and Fascism. In 1935, he wrote the exposé *War Is a Racket*, a trenchant condemnation of the profit motive behind warfare. His views on the subject are summarized in the following passage from the November 1935 issue of the socialist magazine *Common Sense*:

I spent 33 years and four months in active military service and during that period I spent most of my time as a high class muscle man for Big Business, for Wall Street and the bankers. In short, I was a racketeer; a gangster for capitalism. I helped make Mexico and especially Tampico safe for American oil interests in 1914. I helped make Haiti and Cuba a decent place for the National City Bank boys to collect revenues in. I helped in the raping of half a dozen Central American republics for the benefit of Wall Street. I helped purify Nicaragua for the International Banking House of Brown Brothers in 1902–1912. I brought light to the Dominican Republic for the American sugar interests in 1916. I helped make Honduras right for the American fruit companies in 1903. In China in 1927 I helped see to it that Standard Oil went on its way unmolested. Looking back on it, I might have given Al Capone a few hints. The best he could do was to operate his racket in three districts. I operated on three continents.

In November 1934, Butler claimed the existence of a political conspiracy by business leaders to overthrow President Roosevelt, a series of allegations that came to be known in the media as the Business Plot. A special committee of the House of Representatives headed by Representatives John W. McCormack of Massachusetts and Samuel Dickstein of

New York, who was later alleged to have been a paid agent of the NKVD, heard his testimony in secret. The McCormack–Dickstein committee was a precursor to the House Committee on Un-American Activities.

In November 1934, Butler told the committee that one Gerald P. MacGuire told him that a group of businessmen, supposedly backed by a private army of 500,000 ex-soldiers and others, intended to establish a fascist dictatorship. Butler had been asked to lead it, he said, by MacGuire, who was a bond salesman with Grayson M–P Murphy & Co. The *New York Times* reported that Butler had told friends that General Hugh S. Johnson, former head of the National Recovery Administration, was to be installed as dictator, and that the J.P. Morgan banking firm was behind the plot. Butler told Congress that MacGuire had told him the attempted coup was backed by three million dollars, and that the 500,000 men were probably to be assembled in

Washington, D.C. the following year. All the parties alleged to be involved publicly said there was no truth in the story, calling it a joke and a fantasy.

In its report to the House, the committee stated that, while "no evidence was presented... to show a connection... with any fascist activity of any European country... [t]here was no question that these attempts were discussed, were planned, and might have been placed in execution..." and that "your committee was able to verify all the pertinent statements made by General Butler, with the exception of the direct statement about the creation of the organisation. This, however, was corroborated in the correspondence of MacGuire with his principal, Robert Sterling Clark...."

No prosecutions or further investigations followed, and historians have questioned whether or not a coup was actually contemplated. Historians have not reported any independent evidence apart from Butler's report on what MacGuire told him. One of these, Hans Schmidt, says MacGuire was an "inconsequential trickster". The news media dismissed the plot, with a *New York Times* editorial characterizing it as a "gigantic hoax". When the committee's final report was released, the *Times* said the committee "purported to report that a two-month investigation had convinced it that General Butler's story of a Fascist march on Washington was alarmingly true" and "... also alleged that definite proof had been found that the much publicized Fascist march on Washington, which was to have been led by Major Gen. Smedley D. Butler, retired, according to testimony at a hearing, was actually contemplated". The individuals involved all denied the existence of a plot.

Upon his retirement, Butler bought a home in Newtown Square, Pennsylvania, where he lived with his wife. In June 1940, he checked himself into the hospital after becoming sick a few weeks earlier. His doctor described his illness as an incurable condition of the upper gastro-intestinal tract that was probably cancer. His family remained by his side, even bringing his new car so he could see it from the window. He never had a chance to drive it. On June 21, 1940, Smedley Butler died at Naval Hospital, Philadelphia.

The funeral was held at his home, attended by friends and family as well as several politicians, members of the Philadelphia police force and officers of the Marine Corps. He was buried at Oaklands Cemetery in West Goshen Township, Pennsylvania. Since his death in 1940, his family has maintained his home as it was when he died, including a large quantity of memorabilia he had collected throughout his varied career.

4

Made in the USA
Middletown, DE
03 November 2022

14082555R00066